Money Academy for Couples

Get Out of Debt. Fix Your Budget.
Stop Arguing About Money.

NEAL FRANKLE

Certified Financial Planner®

Copyright Notice:

Copyright © Neal Frankle, 2009 All rights reserved.

No part of this publication may be reproduced or transmitted in any form or by any means, mechanical or electronic, including photocopying and recording, or by any information storage and retrieval system, without permission in writing from the publisher.

Legal Notice:

While all attempts have been made to verify information provided in this publication, neither the Authors assumes any responsibility for errors, omissions, or contrary interpretation of the subject matter herein.

This publication is not intended for use as a source of legal, business, investment, tax or accounting advice. The Publisher wants to stress that the information contained herein may be subject to varying state and/or local laws or regulations. All users are advised to retain competent counsel to determine what state and/or local laws or regulations may apply to the user's particular business.

The Purchaser or Reader of this publication assumes responsibility for the use of these materials and information. Adherence to all applicable laws and regulations, federal, state, and local governing professional licensing, business practices, advertising, and all other aspects of doing business in the United States or any other jurisdiction is the sole responsibility of the Purchaser or Reader.

The Authors assume no responsibility or liability whatsoever on the behalf of any Purchaser or Reader of these materials. Any perceived slights of specific people or organizations are unintentional.

Dedication

To Mimi, Rinat, Mor and Maya.
You taught me everything I know that's worth knowing.

Table of Contents

Introduction
Money Academy for Couples

Arguing with your spouse or partner about money can be just about the most stressful, frustrating situation for anyone in a relationship.

I probably don't need to convince you of this. 50% of all married couples divorce, and 90% of them report that the main reason was money.

The good news is, you don't have to argue about money anymore, and disagreements about money don't need to threaten your relationship. You and your partner can work together to repair your finances and your relationship -- and have fun doing it.

Hi, Neal Frankle here with Money Academy for Couples. I'm a certified financial planner, and I've been helping couples with their finances for over 25 years. I'm delighted to be on this journey with you and your partner toward improving your financial situation.

Who am I to tell you about money and relationships?

Even though I'm a financial adviser, I have known what it is to live in complete financial fear. Both my parents died by the time I reached age 17. My mother died of cancer and my father died in an airplane crash two years later. For a short time, I bounced around from one friend's house to another. I never slept underneath a highway overpass, but it felt like I did.

I was frightened and angry. I grew up with a lot of emotional and financial fear. Those **fears didn't subside even when I had my own family** and started making money. Even after I made a great deal of money, those fears remained

To make a long story short, I graduated college, asked the woman of my dreams to marry me (she said yes), and started working. Having a family and income of my own solved some of my problems – but not all of them.

When we got married, **my wife had very little experience dealing with finances**, and we had very different views on what was and what was not a good way to spend.

She wasn't extravagant but she wanted to enjoy life. I was still living in financial fear and wanted to save everything we possibly could.

Disagreements turned into arguments. We were on opposite sides of the street when it came to money, and it was causing huge problems in our relationship.

The fun was gone. Unkind words were exchanged. I grew suspicious of the way she spent money, so I became controlling. She felt that I had taken away her happiness, freedom, friends and life. She was so depressed that she didn't know what to do.

She wanted to spend money we didn't have – and I didn't want to spend the money that we did have. She wasn't being responsible and I wasn't being loving. How did it ever get that bad?

It was awful!

Over a twenty-year period, my wife and I learned how to solve these problems, and that's what I'm going to share with you.

Having more money isn't going to solve financial problems entirely. The key is achieving a healthy balance with your money. I am going to show you how to get balanced and improve your financial situation.

I've spent a lot of time developing this program and putting in everything I know to help you stop struggling, fighting and arguing about money. But there is one thing that this program won't do, and that is to manipulate you or your partner.

In other words, if you bought this workbook in order to make your partner think exactly the way you do, then this program is not going to work for you.

Let's go through the purpose of Money Academy for Couples.

My years of experience as a financial advisor working with couples have taught me that in order to build a successful partnership, couples must work not only on good communication and relationship skills, but also on mastering a basic set of financial principles that will keep them out of financial trouble and out of debt. Therefore, my goals for students of Money Academy for Couples are:

1. **To improve communication.** Good communication is essential to solving financial disagreements. Some couples never talk about money. Others scream about it – that's not talking either. I am going to give you and your partner a way to discuss and fix disagreements rather than fight about and/or ignore the subject. Communication is a key ingredient of what this course is about.

2. **To help identify your goals.** You and your partner may each have different financial goals. There's nothing wrong with that. But we want to be clear about what your goals are and how important they are so that you can prioritize. We're going to go through an exercise that does just that.

3. **To help you and your partner find common ground** and identify the things that you do agree on. We will explore the ideas you share so that you can build on those successes and strengths.

4. **To take an honest look at what is and isn't working financially.** This is important because if you're not going to be honest, you're not going to be able to improve the things that really need work.

5. **To learn how to fix what's not working.** I'm going to talk to you about the basics -- the true foundation of how money works, including credit, debt, credit cards, and more that you may be struggling with. We're going to go through the basics of how money works to give you and your partner a foundation for decision-making that is based on facts.

I've got no vested interest. I'm not just in your corner, and I'm not just in your partner's corner either. I'm in both of your corners. Together, we're going to look at the truth, solve problems and build a better financial future for you both.

There are going to be a number of solutions that will be available to you. However, my job isn't to impose a solution on you. My job is to show you what the options are and to help you, together with your partner, determine what the best decision is.

After you go through these modules and do the work, you will absolutely make progress towards your financial goals. And you will be able to measure your goals so that you see how far you've come. I also want you to share and celebrate those successes.

My promises to you:

1. You will identify what changes need to be made in order to improve your present financial situation.
2. You will make progress and be able to measure it.
3. You will also understand what adjustments need to be made going forward.

What are my goals?

1. **To guide you toward a stronger financial situation.**

   I guarantee that after you go through these modules and do the homework, you're going to have a stronger financial situation. There's no two ways about it.

2. **To help you and your partner build a stronger relationship.**

   As I said in the beginning, one of the main reasons people fight is money. If you can stop arguing about finances, you will have given yourself a huge head start toward a better relationship.

So, there is a lot at stake here.

What am I asking from you?

Go through the exercises. They're not that difficult. After each exercise, take time to discuss it with your partner so that you'll be able to work together going forward.

Have an open mind. If you are already of the mind that you've done everything you need to do, that you don't need to change anything and you have nothing to learn, then this course will be of no use to you.

Be willing to compromise. At the end of the day, no one gets everything. Remember what Mick Jagger said: "You can't always get what you want."

But the song goes on to say: "If you try sometimes, you get what you need."

I promise that if you do the work, **you will get the most important things that you need.** But you need to compromise. You're not going to get everything you want. But you're going to get a lot more than you ever expected -- a tremendous relationship and an improved financial situation. Won't that feel better? Isn't that more important than a great car or an expensive trip?

And you're not going to give up everything. This is not about denying yourself. **This is about compromising as an individual so you have more as a couple.** We're going to discover many ways for you to do just that. But it's essential that you take action on the principles you learn.

It's useless to learn something and never practice it. This program is going to give you practical step-by-step instructions on how you can take action and really get your financial situation on track.

This is not one of those programs that only talks about fair fighting and communication. Of course that's an important component. But if you only learn how to fight fair and communicate, you won't learn how to take action to improve your situation. Who cares if you're fighting fairly when you're going bankrupt?

I am going to give you direct exercises to improve your situation, plus ways to get rid of the anxiety, worry, fights and anger around money. This program will show you how to communicate and how to get unstuck. It is all about you and your relationship moving forward and having a better time while you're on the earth. Right now. Today.

So, here's the deal. I'd like you right now to make a commitment that you're going to be open-minded, willing to learn and compromise with respect to this material. Promise to go through these exercises together, discuss them and take action.

I'd like you to make that commitment right now. In fact, here is the letter I'd like you to copy and sign.

Please take a moment to copy this letter. Sign it and give it to your partner now.

Money Academy for Couples – Agreement
(Please write this out by hand)

I, _____ promise to go through all the exercises contained in Money Academy for Couples together with _____. I further promise to do so with an open mind, an eagerness to learn and willingness to compromise.

Signed:

_____

Date:

_____

If you can't make those commitments to each other, you might as well just close down now. Give this book to someone else who can use it. The course won't be any good to you.

But if you do make this commitment and actually follow through, which I know you can and I know you will, you'll see how powerful the results are.

Let's get started.

Part I:
Improving Communication

Chapter One:
Working Together and Communicating as a Couple

Being part of a couple can be a tremendously joyful, fulfilling experience, but no relationship is without its challenges. I created Money Academy for Couples because I have seen that most couples will experience conflict related to financial disagreements at some point or other. But I'm here to tell you that disagreement of any kind, financial or otherwise, is completely normal and to be expected.

Before you became one half of a couple, you probably spent the majority of your life as a single, self-sufficient individual. You formulated your own opinions, principles and behaviors in ways that aligned with your desires for your safety, health and happiness.

When you married or entered into a committed relationship with shared finances, you suddenly weren't the only person behind the wheel anymore. You had a partner to share decisions with. The tricky part is that before meeting you, your partner was also busy being an individual and formulating his or her own beliefs and habits about how to spend money. After beginning your relationship, you and your partner may have discovered that your financial philosophies are a bit or perhaps extremely different.

Let me repeat: It's completely normal to disagree. Of course you won't see eye-to-eye on everything. Every couple is made up of two distinct individuals who got a lot of practice at being their

> *It's completely normal to disagree.*

own bosses before entering into a relationship. Challenges and conflicts are to be expected.

The good news is that there's hope. You can learn to work through your disagreements and come out stronger as an individual and as a couple.

The types of money disagreements that couples experience are probably infinite -- at any rate, too numerous to list here. Regardless of what your conflict is, you can still learn from the basic principles of the modules in this book. But along the way, it will be essential that you practice communicating and working together as a couple..

Money is an emotional trigger. You're bound to get a little hot under the collar at times. And while I'm no Dr. Phil, I have to stress that it's crucial that you remain calm when you least want to be.

Here are a few guidelines to help you get started:

1. **Listen to your partner.** Now that you're in a committed relationship, decisions can't be made solely based on your desires anymore. You need to try your hardest to hear your partner out and understand where she is coming from.

2. **Prove that you listened.** A good way to show your partner that you care and that you're really listening is to repeat what he's just said. You might say something like: "If I heard you correctly, you just said that it upsets you when I make a large purchase without consulting you. Is that right?"

3. **Be patient.** Don't start making a new point until a) You've asked your partner if he has finished his, and b) You've proven that you listened.

4. **Be clear about your own beliefs.** When it's your turn to talk, remember to be honest. Any lack of honesty can further complicate things down the road.

5. **Be respectful and keep an open mind.** Learning to work with your partner is not about one person being right and the other being wrong. You are both individuals and entitled to the way you feel. But you're also a team now, which means that together you must try

your hardest to arrive at the solution that will increase your shared happiness. Remember to be open to new ideas and compromises, and to always treat your partner with the respect she deserves.

 This is not going to be easy to do, and you'll probably forget these steps just when you need them most. Don't worry. Do the best you can. Practice. It's OK to do it wrong, but don't give up. This is the key to implementing all the ideas that I'll be presenting in the remainder of the book.

Let me give you an example of how these guidelines can work.

Jim and Mary have been married for two years and have a recurring argument. Jim wants to withdraw $10,000 from their emergency savings account for a month-long trip to South America. Travel is one of the couple's mutual interests, and one of the things that initially drew them together. But Mary, who describes herself as more prudent with finances than Jim, wants to keep the $10,000 exactly where it is -- in emergency savings. Both Mary and Jim are in good health and have steady jobs, but Mary still feels more comfortable knowing they have a cushion in case anything should happen. And, Mary has another reason for wanting to keep the money in emergency savings: She opened and fully funded the account prior to marrying Jim. Mary is committed to Jim and their life together, but on a certain level she still feels like the emergency savings, and the decision to spend it, are hers alone.

Whenever Jim brings up the South America trip, Mary immediately becomes defensive and irritated. She doesn't hear Jim out, and she's not completely honest about the ownership she feels of the money. Jim gets frustrated too and doesn't understand why Mary wouldn't want to spend their money on an activity that they'll both enjoy. He assumes that she isn't interested in traveling with him anymore, and he wonders if their marriage was a mistake.

When I look at this situation, there are several things that seem wrong. First, neither Mary nor Jim is really listening to each other. Instead of showing Jim that she understands his point of view, Mary is too focused on defending her own viewpoints. And Jim is making assumptions about Mary's wishes and not putting enough effort into understanding what her desires really are (although it sounds like Mary is also not being honest about what she wants). Jim and Mary's current styles of communication aren't benefiting either partner, and they're certainly not making any progress toward reconciling this disagreement and reaching a solution that makes them both happy.

Here's an example of a more productive way for this conversation to take place:

Jim:
Mary, I'd like us to take out some of our savings and go on a trip to South America. How do you feel about that?

Mary:
To be honest, I'd rather not withdraw from the emergency savings account. I really feel much better knowing that we have a cushion to fall back on in case one of us lost our job or got sick.

Jim:
I think I understand you. You're saying that keeping the money in savings makes you feel more secure. Is that right?

Mary:
Yes. Also, I started that account before we were married. I know that we're a couple now, but I still feel some ownership of the account.

Jim:
I understand. You worked hard to earn that money, and you sacrificed to save it. So you still feel like you get to call the shots with the account.

Mary:
I do feel that way, but that's not really the way I want things to be in our relationship. I want us to learn how to prioritize and make decisions together. Thanks for understanding how I feel, though.

Jim:
I want us to be able to make decisions together too, and I also want us to enjoy our life together and do a fun activity that we'll both love, like the South America trip. When you weren't excited about the trip at first, I thought that meant that you didn't want to travel anymore. But now I think I understand what you're really thinking.

Mary:
No, I do want to keep traveling with you. But I also want us to have back-up money.

Jim:
I understand that now. So, what should we do?

I know it sounds like I'm asking you to morph from Fred and Wilma Flintstone to Mother Theresa and Wayne Dyer.

It's not going to happen overnight, but you do need to make a commitment to the idea of open and fair communication.

Let's look at this new improved exchange and break it down.

The conversation could not be more different from the initial description of Mary and Jim's problem. Both repeated what the other said to prove that they were listening, and Mary was more honest about her beliefs and feelings. Neither became defensive, made assumptions or pointed fingers -- they simply stated their viewpoints and attempted to understand each other in order to move on toward finding a solution to their problem.

Establish trust through respectful communication.

Having an open, honest conversation like the one above is just the beginning. After establishing trust through respectful communication, the next step is to work out a solution that makes sense for the couple.

Keep the guidelines for effective communication in mind as you read the rest of the book. You and your partner will go through exercises that teach you how to prioritize and develop good financial habits, but open communication will be key to the success of your joint efforts.

SUMMARY

Chapter One:
Working Together and
Communicating as a Couple

- Disagreements between couples (about money or anything else) are completely normal
- Many partners have different beliefs and habits about money before they get married, so it's no wonder that disagreements come up after marriage
- Each partner is an individual and entitled to his or her opinion, but now that they are a team, both parties must make every effort to understand each other and come together to find a solution that is in the best interest of both
- Open, honest communication is key to working together as a couple
- Guidelines for effective communication:
  - ▷ Listen
  - ▷ Prove you listened by repeating what your partner says
  - ▷ Be patient
  - ▷ Be clear about your own beliefs
  - ▷ Be respectful and keep an open mind

Part II:
Identifying Your Goals

Chapter Two:
The Most Important Question

Here's a question for you that may seem a little strange, but is actually the most important question I could ask.

Ready? Here it is:

What is important about money to you?

I can imagine that nobody has ever asked you that question before – but it's super important.

The reason it's so important is because it's the yardstick by which you measure whether or not you're financially on track.

Let me give you an example.

If you asked me what's important about money to me, I would say my family and being of service to other people and my community. Now, if you knew those were my values, you could see if my financial behavior was consistent or inconsistent with those values.

So, if I told you that I try to help others in the work I do, I'm not in debt and I have life insurance, those behaviors would be consistent with my values.

However, if I said, "Well, I drive a Lamborghini that I can't afford and I have three homes that I'm almost being foreclosed on and I go to Vegas every other week," there would be a total disconnect between what I describe my values to be and how I live.

This is why the question is so important. In fact, I'll tell you another thing.

I don't care how much money you have. **You'll never be happy unless your behavior is consistent with your goals and values.** There are plenty of examples of very wealthy people with tons of money who are just miserable. The reason? Their behavior is not consistent with their values and goals. How can people ever hope to attain the success and happiness they desire if their actions don't match up with their values?

Let's go back to my example. Remember, I said what's important is my family, charity and my community. But let's say I exhibit all the behaviors that run counter to those values. Instead of making donations or paying my kids' college tuition, most of my money goes towards a collection of sports cars and a lavish home.

I know exactly what I need to do. I may not want to change my behaviors, but I know what I need to do in order to be consistent with my values -- in order to be happy.

> *Maximize your long-term joy.*

That's an important point to keep in mind. **This exercise isn't about maximizing your short-term happiness. It's all about maximizing your long-term joy.**

If you have debt, you're not going to get out of it instantly. It will take work. The next several modules will help you significantly toward that end. But right now, I'm not worried about your debt. I'm interested in your financial behaviors.

Starting today, what behavior are you going to change? You may not be able to turn this around overnight. If you are involved in a business that is losing money, you may have to wind it down. That takes time. But there must be some changes you can make today that will have a real impact. What are they?

If you're involved in a social group that you have to extricate yourself from (because you spend too much money as a result of being in that group), you may be able to do it quickly. If so, don't make excuses for yourself -- move quickly.

This is about you taking significant action in ways that will make your behavior more consistent with your goals and values -- and much happier.

Do the exercises for this module individually.

Once you've each gone through them individually, share your answers with each other.

It'll be a great conversation. You may learn that you both have the same values, but simply express them differently.

What's Important About Money To You?

Directions: Complete this exercise individually and share with your partner.

When you think about it, what is important about money to you?

How does your financial behavior support your values?

How does your financial behavior conflict with your values?

What are you going to do differently?

When are you going to start?

SUMMARY

Chapter Two: The Most Important Question

- One of the most important questions you can ask yourself and your partner is, "What is important about money to you?"
- You'll never be happy unless your behavior is consistent with your values and goals.
- By making sure your behavior is in step with your goals, you will maximize your long-term happiness.

Part III:
Finding Common Ground

Chapter Three:
Finding Common Ground

When your goal is to build a strong relationship, it's critical to have a solid financial foundation. The way to build that strong foundation is to look for common ground.

The first question to ask yourself is, **what do you like about your partner's financial behavior?** Try to think of at least one thing that you like about his or her financial habits. For example, if someone is very frugal, at least you can say that she doesn't overspend. If someone spends too much, at least you can say he takes you out to nice places or buys you nice things. So, find something nice to say about the other person's financial behavior.

The next question is, **"What can you do to make your shared financial life stronger and better?"**

How will your partner answer these questions? What do you think your partner would say about what you should (or could) do to make your financial lives better?

Are you earning less than you should? Do you have to handle debt better? Are you disorganized around money and paperwork? Do you stress and argue quite a bit? What do you need to do better? What will your partner say you need to improve?

Of course, the last question is, **what bugs you about your partner's financial behavior?**

This is the question you've been waiting for, right? What is it that you'd like to see your partner change? How do *those* issues impact you?

We're trying to find common ground -- not just positive things you agree on, but things that you both agree have to be worked on.

Why is this important?

First, you're going to identify things you need to change about yourself.

Next, you're going to communicate what you would like your partner to change. In doing this, you will be honest and vulnerable. That's going to enhance your relationship.

Also, you will both find agreement on what needs to change and when.

Admitting your own challenges will help you realize that your partner isn't the only one whose behavior needs to improve. You have things to work on too.

Being honest about your own problems also allows your partner to be a little bit more open.

 **Think about it. Would you rather have a talk with Oprah or be interrogated by the Gestapo?**

Be kind, honest and vulnerable. This way, your partner can be honest about what they need to work on without fear of being attacked. This exercise will help you, but it's very important to do it gently. The best way to invite someone to be honest about themselves is to be honest about your own failings first.

Find the common ground in things that you like about the other person, the things that you need to change about yourself and the things that you would like the other person to change too.

Spend a few minutes and talk this exercise over before going on to the next module.

Find Common Ground Module

Directions: Complete this exercise individually and discuss with your partner.

1. What do you like about your partner's financial behavior?

2. What do you need to do differently in order to make your financial life better?

3. What would your partner say? Which financial behaviors would they like to see you change?

4. What bugs you about your partner's financial behavior? What would you like to see them change?

5. How do your financial behaviors negatively impact yourself and your partner?

6. How do your partner's issues negatively impact you and your partner?

SUMMARY

Chapter Three: Finding Common Ground

- A solid financial foundation is critical to building a strong relationship.
- The way to build a strong foundation is to look for common ground.
- Common ground includes things that you are your partner agree are already working, and things that you agree need work.

Part IV:
Understand What's Working (and What's Not)

Chapter Four:
Dollarize Your Behavior

Let's find out what your financial behavior costs you and your partner in both money and time. I call this "dollarizing your behavior."

It's easy to identify the cost of your behavior. If, for example, you go out to eat five times a week and you're spending $300 a week doing so, that's $1,200 a month. The cost of eating out is $1,200 a month PLUS the interest on any credit card debt this spending creates.

But what if you're spending too much time? Again, I'm not trying to say that you shouldn't spend time doing things you like. But let's just take a look and see what it costs you in time and money when you're engaged in some activity that you're doing maybe a little bit too much of.

Let's say you spend 10 hours a month "surfing" on EBay -- and you do it "for fun."

But let's assume that you're also in debt. And, let's assume that you could spend that same 10 hours a month earning $25 an hour. You could take a job like mowing lawns on the weekends or whatever it takes to get out of debt.

How much does your time cost?

So, in this case, the "cost" of your fun is $25 per hour for 10 hours - or $250 a month. That's $3,000 a year.

- 10 hours/month on Ebay
- Average hourly wage $25/hour
- Total Monthly Cost $250
- Over $3,000/year

That's a lot of money – especially when you are in debt. And the reason that I'm bringing this up is because every time you say "yes" to one thing (like surfing EBay), you're saying "no" to something else -- like paying off your debt.

What I'd like you each to do now please is "dollarize" your behavior.

How much does your your time cost?
Let's "dollarize" it.

Directions: Please go through this individually. Then come back, discuss it and see if there is something that you need to do to make a change. If there are changes that need to be made, make sure you become accountable to your partner on an ongoing basis.

How much money do you overspend each month? _____
(If you aren't sure of the amount, I'll help you figure that out in the next module)

How much time do you spend daily?
- Watching T.V   _____
- Web surfing   _____
- Shopping   _____
- Other   _____

Total Time Wasted Each Day   _____
Total Time Wasted Each Month   _____

Could you spend that time earning money that you really need?

If yes, how much could you earn during that time?

So how much does your behavior cost you every month? (Number of hours spent times the amount you could earn per hour.)

What are you going to do differently? Starting when?

Who are you going to be accountable to?

How often?

SUMMARY

Chapter Four: Dollarize Your Behavior

- It's important to track the cost of your behavior, especially if you are in debt.
- Saying "yes" to one activity almost always means saying "no" to another.

Chapter Five:
Track Your Spending

We're now going to talk about spending and debt. These are huge issues that plague lots of people, but we are going to nip them in the bud. With a little work, these issues won't be problems for you or your partner any more.

It is critically important to track and look at your spending. I'll give you two stories that illustrate the importance of it.

First, I met a couple many years ago that were worth $4 million. They were making $400,000 a year but couldn't afford to retire because they were also spending $600,000 a year. Neither of them was tracking spending, so they never knew why they were having problems and never realized why their assets were depleting in value. All this couple had to do was look at their spending and see.

Second, I met another couple that was having trouble with expenses. The husband was bringing home $5,000 a month, and he and his wife told me that they spent $3,000 a month. With $2,000 left over from his paycheck each month, I figured that over a year they should have saved $24,000, right?

So I asked the couple: "Where's the $24,000 you saved last year?"

They said, "No. We didn't save $24,000. Actually, we spent more than we earned. We racked up $12,000 in credit card debt."

Were they really spending $5,000 each month? Nope. They were spending $5,000 plus $1,000 a month. Since the couple spent $12,000 more than they earned in the prior year, that works out to $1,000 a month. They were spending $6,000 a month.

That's pretty important information to have. That couple thought they only spent $3,000 a month when in fact they spent $6,000. If you want to retire and you don't know where your money's gone, how can you ever possibly retire?

In my 25 years' experience, I've found that knowing the total of what you spend each month is the most important information you can have. This will help you in two ways: First, you'll get a stronger financial footing. Second, you'll stop fighting about money. It's going to make a huge difference for you.

Now, some people disagree. They argue that you have to mark down every single item you spend money on. It's not really true.

It might be helpful if you write down everything, but it's not critical and it's not even enough. You still have to have the one overall number that represents your monthly expenses. This will help you see the forest for the trees.

The good news is that you can track your spending in five minutes a month. But before I tell you how to do that, I will tell you one other thing: If you're not willing to spend the five minutes a month to track your overall spending, then you're sure as heck not going to spend the two, three hours a week it's going to take you to track every single thing. If you're going to do nothing else, do this one thing. It will make a huge difference. I guarantee it.

Ready to learn about the "5 Minute A Month Method"? Is the suspense killing you?

Well ... hold your horses.

Before we get started, I just have **one more** question. Don't share your answer with your partner yet.

What do you think you spend every month on average, including the mortgage and rent and travel and fixing the refrigerator and fixing the roof and every other expense? **What do you think you spend every month on average?** Take a second, write it down on a piece of paper and again, don't share your answer with your spouse.

Whatever answer you gave, you're probably way off.

In fact, most people spend at least 30% more than they think they spend. Let me show you how to find out if I'm right by introducing you to the "5 Minute A Month" method.

To implement this great tool, all you have to do is look at your bank statements. They will tell you exactly what you really spend every month.

The 5-Minute A Month Method

In fact, what I'd like you to do is stop for a minute and get your last 12 bank statements. If you can't or you don't have them handy, ask the bank to resend them right away.

Remember, the goal is to know exactly how much you spend every month on average. For now, I don't care how you spend the money. By first knowing exactly how much you spend on average each month, you'll be in a good position to make smart decisions about how to spend money later. But until you know your total monthly average spending, it's impossible to put individual expenditures in proportion. You have to know if you are living within your means or not in order to know what you can and cannot afford. That's the mistake that most people and financial authors make. They forget about the big picture.

Again, **the way to know exactly what you spend each month is to simply look at your checking account statement.** On your statement, you'll see one number that shows you the total withdrawals for the month. Look at Figure 1. Do you see the "Other Withdrawals" of $5,882.61? That tells me how much was spent from this account that month. That's the number you are looking for.

This number includes payments to your credit card companies and all the cash you withdrew to play the ponies or to pay for the cleaning person. That's what you spend.

What I'd like you to do is get the last 12 bank statements and I'll help you create a spreadsheet so you can keep tabs on what your *average* spending is.

Your Account at a Glance	
Beginning Balance	259.55
Checks Paid	0.00
Other Withdrawals	5882.61
Deposits	5963.00
Ending Balance	339.94

Figure 1

This is a foolproof system. It's easy and quick.

Before you calculate your monthly average, I need to ask you a few questions:

1. **Do you write checks to pay for all of your expenses from one checking account?** Good. But if you pay bills from more than one checking account you must simplify and use one checking account if at all possible. Having multiple accounts makes it almost impossible to track spending and leads to chaos.

    (If you simply must have more than one account because your spouse or partner insists on it, or because you have a small business or you set up different accounts for special purchases, just make sure you don't move money back and forth between accounts. In this case, run the following exercise on both accounts to determine what you really spend, on average, each month in each account.)

2. **Do you earn and spend cash?**
    Remember, the idea is to *know* how much it costs you to live each month. If you earn and spend cash, it's off the radar screen. It doesn't go through the checking account, so this exercise won't take it into account unless you take an extra step. The solution for this is to simply add it to your spending number. You'll see how this works in the spreadsheet below.

3. **Does your credit card debt go up or down?**
    If your credit card balance goes up, that means that you are financing your lifestyle with debt. In other words, you spend all you make and then some. Any increases in credit card balance must be added to your spending number. Any decrease in credit card balance is deducted from your spending balance. This is because a payment

to decrease an outstanding credit card balance (over and above the monthly charges) isn't an ongoing expense. Again, see how this works in the spreadsheet below.

4. Does a business (or someone else) pay for some of your personal expenses?

Take the example of an employer-provided automobile. The business might provide this now, but even if you didn't have the business or job, you'd probably still need a car. That means if you didn't have the job, your expenses would go up.

Since the goal is to calculate what it really costs you to live, add back in any expenses that someone else pays for that you would have to pay for if they stopped providing it.

5. What if you had an unusually high expense one month?

If you and your partner incur an unusual expense like a car purchase or a kitchen remodel, it would be a mistake to include those numbers to calculate your average monthly spending. Simply take those expenses out of the monthly number before you calculate the average.

However, you should have other accounts that you use to help save the money for these unusual expenses. In other words, if you know you will need a car every seven years and you spend $21,000 on the car, you should put $3,000 aside each year for that purpose. On a monthly basis, that works out to be $3,000/12, or $250 a month. This $250 should be included in your monthly average for spending.

Now, we're ready to get to work!

A. Get the last 12 months worth of bank statements. Each statement will provide a number on the first page that tells you the total withdrawals for the month. This is the only number we care about.

B. Create a spreadsheet that lists the total withdrawal figures for the last 12 months. It should look something like the rabbit hunter, Elmer's (shown below). Make sure to include information on any cash earned and spent (that didn't go through the ATM), personal expenses paid by others and credit card balance changes.

Date	Total With-drawal	Cash earned & spent (not ATM withdraw-als)	Personal Expenses paid by business or Uncle Elmo	Credit Card Balance Changes	Total Cost of Living
8-Jan	$4,503				$4,503.00
8-Feb	$5,200				$5,200.00
8-Mar	$9,789		$1,000	($6,000)	$4,789.00
8-Apr	$12,987				$12,987.00
8-May	$3,276	$700			$3,976.00
8-Jun	$4,678				$4,678.00
8-Jul	$4,921		$300		$5,221.00
8-Aug	$6,783				$6,783.00
9-Sep	$4,075	$600			$4,675.00
8-Oct	$4,998				$4,998.00
8-Nov	$4,564			$400	$4,964.00
8-Dec	$5,287				$5,287.00
9-Jan	$5,253				$5,253.00
9-Feb	$5,576				$5,576.00
9-Mar	$5,542				$5,542.00

Notice that the spending in TOTAL WITHDRAWALS was higher in some months than in other months. That's normal.

For example, look at the total spending for April 2008. It's very high at $12,987. That was because Elmer paid property taxes that month. Notice that Elmer's expenses were also a bit higher in August of 2008 – he spent $6,783. That was because Elmer's car needed repairs. Again, it makes no difference why Elmer spent a bit more that month. In fact, the whole reason that we calculate a 12 month average is to smooth out the expenses that are not incurred each month. It's normal for some months to be higher than others.

In May and September, Elmer earned $700 and $600 cash respectively working for his brother. Elmer spent all that money on rabbit food (to lure Bugs), so he must add that as an expense. Why? He would have bought the rabbit food anyway, even if he hadn't earned the cash.

In March and July, his business picked up some travel costs that Elmer would have had to spend even if his employer wouldn't have covered them. He adds those too.

But in March, he paid down his credit card balance by $6,000. That wasn't an expense even though it came out of his bank account. It wasn't a cost of living. He paid off debt, which is a good thing. As a result, it gets deducted from the expense column.

You are going to have a chance to try this yourself when we get to the exercises at the end of the chapter.

C. Calculate average monthly spending.

Date	Total Cost of Living	12 month Average
Jan-08	$4,503	
Feb-08	$5,200	
Mar-08	$4,789	
Apr-08	$12,987	
May-08	$3,976	
Jun-08	$4,678	
Jul-08	$5,221	
Aug-08	$6,783	
Sep-09	$4,675	
Oct-08	$4,998	
Nov-08	$4,964	
Dec-08	$5,287	
Jan-09	$5,253	$5,734
Feb-09	$5,576	$5,766
Mar-09	$5,542	$5,828

You can calculate your 12-month average in one of two ways. The easiest way is to let the computer do it for you. Use the AVERAGE function in Microsoft Excel. If you do not know how to do this, you can do a search for "AVERAGE FUNCTION" in Excel.

If you would rather calculate the old fashioned way, it is also very straightforward. Simply add the previous 12 months' total withdrawals and divide by 12. Do this each month so that you calculate a moving average. In other words, when Elmer does this in January of 2009, he uses January of 2008 through December of 2008. In February, he'll use the data from February of 2008 through January of 2009 to calculate his average.

You can see that in Elmer's case, the 12-month trailing average in January is $5734. In February, it goes up to $5766. Why? Because January 2008 falls off the computation ($4503) and is replaced with February 2008 ($5200).

Once you go through this exercise you will know exactly what it costs you to live, on average, each month. Congratulations! You now have more information than 95% of Americans. Update this spreadsheet each month by recalculating the 12-month average spending.

D. Determine if you are living within your means or not.

Knowing what you spend on average each month will motivate you to now look for ways to cut expenses if that's what you need to do. For example, if you spend $30 week on movies, it might not seem like much. But if your income is $4,500 and you spend $4,600 each month on average, you might see your movie ritual in a different light.

The bottom line is, this exercise is important because it helps you see the big picture and puts everything else in context. It is very important to update this spreadsheet every month. It will take you less than five minutes and is a great use of your time. Once you have this information it will be very easy to make smart spending decisions.

A side benefit is that it will make it very easy for you (as a couple) to eliminate stress around making financial decisions. There is no arguing around the facts, and this exercise will make the facts of your spending crystal clear.

To eliminate stress, arguments, the threat of financial ruin and bankruptcy, you must spend less than you earn. You knew that before you read this. But now, you know what you spend and whether or not you need to cut. And, you will be able to calculate your monthly spending in less than five minutes every month.

After doing this exercise, it's very important to talk it over with your family. I send my spreadsheet to my wife and kids every month, and I suggest you do the same. It's not going to be valuable unless you share the information.

In fact, I'd like you to pull out your calendars and schedule a time right now. Schedule when you're going to update the spreadsheet, and when you're going to discuss it.

Okay. Go ahead and fill out your monthly spending tracker now and calculate your average monthly spending.

Track Your Monthly Spending

Directions: Fill this out individually or with your partner, but be sure to discuss with each other and your family.

1. Set up the "Monthly Spending Tracker" spreadsheet (see example below).

2. Get your checking account statements from the previous 12 months.

3. Note how much cash you earned and spent (if any) that did not go through the checking account. Note any expenses you incurred that other people or businesses pay for. Note any increases or decreases in credit card balances.

4. Input the month/year in column A and the numbers (above) in the appropriate column.

5. Calculate the average amount you spent per month.

6. Schedule a time to update this sheet and discuss the results with your family every month for the rest of your life.

MONTH	Total Withdrawals From Bank Statement	Cash Earned & Spent (Not ATM withdrawals but Cash you received and not deposited in bank...then spent)	Personal expenses paid by someone else	Card card balance change	Calculate Your Average Monthly Spending

SUMMARY

Chapter Five: Track Your Spending

- Knowing the total of what you spend each month is the most important information you can have
- You can track your spending in five minutes a month using the method described in this chapter.

Part V:
How to Fix
What's Not Working

Chapter Six:
Stop Digging Yourself Deeper in Debt

In case you haven't noticed, a very big part of your financial success is tied to your spending and your debt.

Now, believe it or not, there is good debt and bad debt. Sometimes it's hard to tell the difference.

Buying a home could be an example of either good or bad debt. Here's what I mean. Can you afford your mortgage payments? Do you need a 7,500-square-foot home that you can't afford? Or, can you get by with something that's a little bit more reasonable?

So, buying the right home is an example of good debt. Buying the wrong home is an example of bad debt.

What is a clear example of bad debt?

One example is using debt to finance your lifestyle. For example, when you buy a car, you have a choice between a five-year old Toyota and a brand new Bentley. Now, if you can afford the Bentley, go for it. Make sure you pick me up and take me for a ride because I've never been in one.

But if you can't afford the Bentley, don't waste your money. Don't buy a car (or anything) to try to impress someone. You don't need to do that. Be mindful of ways to reduce your expenses because that can help reduce stress.

If you're making $2,000 a month, you can't afford a $700-a-month car payment. You'll never succeed financially if you overspend.

Let's consider investments now.

Please never, ever borrow money to make investments. Let's assume that you could borrow money at 3% and loan it out at 7%. Seems attractive....right?

There are some people who do that and make money, but there is huge risk because sometimes things go wrong.

A good example of how bad this can be is if you borrow money on your house to invest in the stock market.

This is a terrible and dangerous idea. *Never borrow money to make investments.*

Why?

Because even if the stock markets returned 5%, 10%, 15% or 20% last year, there's risk to it. It could lose 30% or 40% next year -- like it did in 2008. If that happens to the market, what is going to happen to you? You've borrowed money which you must repay, but you won't have the money to repay it. Not a good situation for you, my friend.

So if you borrow money to make investments that are risky, you've got to be prepared for the time when the investments don't work out. You must always have a defense plan. Think conservatively, and you will never be overextended or in trouble.

And never, ever borrow money to support your lifestyle. If you spend $3,000 a month to live and you only earn $2,000 a month, you will never, ever survive financially.

You'll always be miserable and in debt. Never, ever get into debt to support your lifestyle.

 **Your spending habits are your key to your financial future.** You have much greater control over your spending habits than your income. It's hard to increase your income significantly, but it's easy to control what you spend.

Let me show you how debt will suffocate your future.

Movies	$100
Lunch	$75
Starbucks	$50
Monthly Total	$225
Annual	$2,700

Figure 2

Let's assume that you go to the movies a few times a month, lunch a few times a week and Starbucks a few times a week. Assume you spend $225 more on these activities than you earn each month.

At the end of the year, that means you spent $2,700 more than you earned. Let's take a look and see what happens to your financial situation over the years.

The first year, you made $25,000 but spent $27,700. Therefore, you have a debt of $2,700. But you've got to pay interest on that debt. Assume interest is $200. So, at the end of the first year, your debt has grown to $2,916.

	Year 1	Year 2	Year 3	Year 4	Year 5
Earn	$25,000	$26,250	$27,563	$28,941	$30,388
Spend	$27,700	$29,085	$30,539	$32,066	$33,670
Difference	-$2,700	-$2,835	-$2,977	-$3,126	-$3,282
Debt	-$2,916	-$6,211	-$9,923	-$14,092	-$18,764

In the second year, you received a raise. You're earning more. Now you earn $26,250. But you're still going out to lunch and Starbucks and the movies, right? And those costs went up too.

Now, you're spending $2,900 each month. So, when you calculate it, your yearly deficit is now $2,835. In year two, you owe $2,835 plus $2,916 and then interest on the sum of those. So, now your debt comes to $6,211 at the end of the second year. This is all because you saw a few movies and had a few coffees and a few lunches that you really couldn't afford.

And five years down the road, look what's happened. You now earn $30,388, but you're spending $33,000 and change. That's $3,200 more than you earned.

And you've got accumulated debt from prior years too. Congratulations, you owe $18,764.

You don't have to have some huge financial blowout to have a huge financial problem.

It's insidious; it starts small but builds up quickly. This is why it's critically important to know how much you spend every month. And we went through that in an earlier module on "Tracking Your Spending in Five Minutes a Month."

If you want to see a picture of how bad it gets, look how quickly and deeply you dig yourself into a hole if you don't watch it.

How Quickly You Fall Into Debt

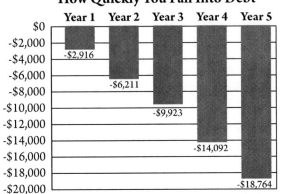

It's scary. And it's a relationship killer. If you want to make sure that your relationship doesn't have a meltdown, make sure this doesn't happen to you. Bottom line, spend less than you earn.

We've agreed that being in the debt pit stinks. We're going to get you out – period.

The first step is to stop digging deeper of course. The next step is to get you out of the ditch.

First, let's calculate the amount you need to cut immediately – it's an easy number to calculate.

Look at how much money you're bringing home. Look at your paycheck, and look at how much you spend on average. And if you see that you're spending more than you bring in, then you know what to do. You've got to cut.

That's easy.

Now, how do you know what to cut?

Well, *this* is when you go back and look through your checks and credit card expenses. If you're spending cash, you look through every single line item. You're going to figure out exactly what you have to do to cut.

If you figure you're earning $2,500 and you're spending $3,000, you've got to cut $500.

I'd like you to go through each of your expenses. If an expense is for something you don't absolutely need, get rid of it.

My suggestion is, do it right now. Right now. Go through your expenses. And if you know you've got to cut $500, let's have at it. Assume you have to cut the karate lessons, pick up the phone and call the studio and cancel the lessons right now.

I know how hard it is because I've done it before. It's tough to cut back when it comes to kids... I know. But in the long run, it's a great lesson for them. **When you do this you are demonstrating responsibility and leadership.** They don't teach that in school, and you can't put a price tag on that lesson.. If it's art lessons, the bowling club, whatever -- pick up the phone and call. It's not as hard as it seems. Just do it.

Don't wait until you *feel* that it's the right thing to do.

If you're in debt, you need to cut right now. Go through each line item and figure out what you've got to cut and start making those cuts immediately before the sun sets today. Take action like you promised me you would.

You don't need any more research. You don't need any more knowledge. You know what to do; you've just got to do it. And you're doing it not only for yourself, but for your family and your partner.

What's next?

Talk to your family. Have a conversation and say, "Look, here's where we are. We're making $3,000 a month. We're spending $4,000 a month. We have to cut because we can't afford it. This is what we're going to do." And make sure that the cuts are across the board and that everybody chips in with the cuts, not just one person -- okay?

I know this isn't easy. But let's look at a similar situation...

Let's say a smoker goes to her doctor. The doctor tells our friend to stop smoking. The doctor knows it's not easy to stop, but warns the smoker that she'll die if she doesn't quit.

If the smoker refuses to stop smoking, you'd think he or she was a fool.

I know this is true because it's exactly what happened to a friend of mine. She had lung cancer and would not stop smoking. As a result, a cancer that could have been survivable probably won't be.

Now debt isn't as deadly as smoking, but it is fatal to your financial health. Every day you wait it makes it more difficult. Take action now.

Don't buy any more books. Don't do any more research. Do the assignment now please.

Remember to talk with your family about it. And make sure that you have an accountability partner. It might be your spouse or somebody else that you trust. Tell them how much you're going to cut and when. Call them now and make a commitment. Call back after you make the cuts and confirm that it's done.

Stop Digging Deeper

Directions: Complete this exercise together.

Do you have any "bad debt"?

What is it?

Did you create it by choice? Or did you have to spend that money? (Example: medical needs)

How are you going to get rid of the bad debt?

Starting when?

Do you have a "deficit disorder" (you spend more than you bring home)?

How much do you earn (take home) each month?

How much do you spend each month on average (from the "Tracking Your Spending in Five Minutes a Month" module)?

How much spending do you need to cut each month?

Easy Ways to Cut Your Spending

Directions: Complete this exercise together.

1. Go through your checking account statements, credit card statements and cash records from the last three months.

2. Highlight those items that you didn't really need to spend money on.

3. Calculate the total.
    (The total must be at least as much as the amount you must cut, as determined by the previous exercise. If not, go through your statements again and find more cuts.

4. How will your life be different once you make these changes?

5. What are you going to do? Are you going to pick up the phone and start cancelling subscriptions, services, etc.? Are you going to make other spending cuts?

6. Starting when?

SUMMARY

Chapter Six: Stop Digging Yourself Deeper in Debt

- Your spending habits are key to your financial future.
- Financial problems usually start small and build up. That's why it's critically important to know how much you spend every month.
- If you're in debt, you must go through each of your expenses to determine what you can cut in order to pull yourself out of a debt pit.

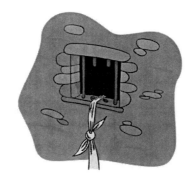

Chapter Seven:
Get Out of Debt

It's time to get you out of the debt pit. Remember that in the last chapter, you and your partner stopped digging deeper. You took steps to stop spending more than you earn. You've done that successfully, and I'm assuming that you're no longer digging yourself in deeper.

So remember, there's no reason to buy more programs, no reason to buy more books at this point, no reason to do lots of research on the Internet. Now is the time for action. You've cut your spending. Now we're ready to get you out of the pit.

The first thing to do is make a list of all your debts.

You need a statement for each of the debts that you have. Get your most recent mortgage statement, your credit card bills, your student loans – everything. Even if you have personal loans at zero interest, get a statement or make one.

(If you don't have statements, call the loan company and get the information. You want to know how much you owe them, including the payments and the interest rate.)

Now I'd like you to fill out your debt inventory.

On the next page, you have a debt inventory spreadsheet. Please fill it out.

Debt Inventory Spreadsheet

Whom do you owe money to?	How Much Do You Currently Owe?	What is the Interest Rate?	What is the Payment Amount?

List whom you owe money to in the first column. The second column is the total amount you owe. The third column is the interest rate that you're paying. And the fourth column is the (monthly) payment amount.

Next, I'd like you to order these from highest interest rate (column 3) to lowest interest rate. You want to see who's charging you the most interest.

Now, you are going to consolidate your debt very, very wisely. Here's what I mean by that: If one credit card is charging you 15%, and another is charging you 10% or 9% or 8%, you can hopefully roll that 15% debt over to another credit card with a lower rate.

If you have credit card debt and you can roll it over to the home equity line or real estate loans, even better. The interest rate will be lower. Of course, you should consult your tax preparer prior to doing this.

But, you always want to roll the highest debt to the lowest debt possible. So if you're going to refinance a house, maybe take a little bit more and pay off that credit card debt, okay? Get rid of high-interest credit cards. They are your number one enemy, your mortal enemy.

A Word about Consolidation Loans

I'm not a huge fan. If you have a loan at 9% and 4% and 7%, and someone else is willing to consolidate them all at 9-1/2% or 10%, that's crazy. You don't need to do that. Consolidate if and only if you reduce the interest rate.

Here's another tip that you may not have thought of.

Let's assume that your current debt costs you 15%. Go to your family and say, "Look, I owe these people money at 15%. I'd like to borrow money from you, pay them off and pay you 7%. And here's my plan to pay you back. Here's how much income I have. Here are my expenses. Here's the extra. You're going to get this money every month automatically. Here's my plan. Here's when it will be paid off."

If you show them a plan for how you're going to pay them, you might just get them to agree – but don't manipulate anyone or make promises you can't keep.

You may have let them down in the past, but you're getting it together now. Tell them you have this program. You're going through it. You want to consolidate your loans.

Now, after you've consolidated the debt to the least-cost loans, the next thing is to go back to the people you still owe money to and bargain with them.

I'd like you to go back to your credit card companies and ask three questions:

1. What can you do to reduce this interest?
2. Is that the best you can do?
3. Can I speak to your supervisor?

No matter what they say, ask these three questions in that order.

If you ask those three questions, believe me, you're going to get some good service. It works wonders, and you're going to have a lot of fun with it.

After you've done that, I want you to go back and update your spreadsheet. Reorder your debts on the sheet, because hopefully you've gotten rid of some of the high-interest loans and rolled them into lower-interest loans.

Now, you've got an updated spreadsheet.

Now you're ready to attack this debt.

Here's what I want you to do. I want you to throw everything you have, your heavy artillery, all the cash you can, at the highest-interest debt, that first line item.

Put all the money you can toward that high-interest debt and make your minimum payments towards all your other debts. Do this until the first debt is paid off. Then, repeat the exercise on the next-highest cost debt.

Now, some people will say that you want to pay off the lowest balance first. And from an emotional standpoint, it might feel better. And if that floats your boat, that's okay with me.

But it's not the best thing to do financially. The best thing to do financially is to attack the highest-interest debt first. And I think that you'll get just as much emotional payoff by seeing that sucker go down and down and down and down very quickly.

In summary, I want you to throw all your money at your highest-interest rate debt and make minimum debt payments toward the other debts. The goal is to kill that debt dragon, and once you do, go on to the next monster. Keep in mind that once the highest debt is paid off, you have that extra money that you were paying them. Put that extra cash toward the next highest debt. Update your spreadsheet each time you pay off a debt.

Attack highest interest debt first.

This is the debt snowball that Dave Ramsey talks about. The money you have available to pay off debt increases just like a snowball.

Why?

Because you are taking the same amount of money and using it to pay off an ever-diminishing amount of debt.

The next thing to do is celebrate your success. I don't want you to go to Vegas. Just give yourself a hug, or do something nice for yourself that's inexpensive. There are a ton of things you can do to celebrate without spending an arm and a leg. Find something and celebrate.

Let me tell you a secret. This entire exercise isn't about being out of debt. This is about stopping bad behavior and focusing on good behavior.

It's a day at a time process. One day at a time, you're going to stop digging yourself into deeper debt. One day at a time, you're going to take action to get out of the debt pit that you've created. And that is success.

You don't have to be debt-free before you celebrate. You should celebrate starting this course because you're taking action. Celebrate when you complete each homework assignment.

You've done something good for yourself and your family. So celebrate your success and talk with your partner about how you're going to do that in an inexpensive manner. Decide together.

Of course, the final advice is to never incur more debt. Remember, you're going to work hard to get out of this debt pit. You know that if you don't work hard to get out of it, your future is going to be very, very difficult.

Don't shame yourself for the past, but don't ever let this happen to you again. And the way you can make sure that doesn't happen is if you do all the other exercises that I've already suggested that you do.

Namely, track your expenses. **The Five Minutes a Month Method** is fantastic. Track your expenses and have meetings with your partner on an ongoing basis to make sure it never happens.

You don't have to get out of debt before you go to the next assignment, but I would strongly suggest you complete all the exercises below before moving on.

Get Out of the Debt Pit

Directions: Complete these exercises together.

Debt Inventory

1. Get all the most recent statements for the debts you have (credit cards, mortgage statements, student loans, etc).

2. Make sure the statement shows the current balance and interest rate being charged.

3. Fill out the enclosed "Debt Inventory Spreadsheet" (shown earlier in this chapter).

How To Get Out Of Debt

1. Can you roll high-interest debt to lower-interest debt? Call the low-interest debt company to find out how. Can you "roll" the debt to someone in your family at a lower rate?
2. Call your creditors to try to get them to reduce your interest rate.

3. Update your "Debt Inventory Spreadsheet".

4. Sort the matrix with the highest-interest rate debt first – it doesn't matter what the balances are.

5. Throw all the money you can every month towards paying off the highest- interest rate debt while making the minimum payments on all the other debts.

6. Once this first high-interest rate debt is paid, apply all the money you can towards the next highest-interest rate debt.

7. Continue this process until all your debt is paid off.

How to Get Out of Debt - Other Resources

Trent Hamm has a wonderful website - www.thesimpledollar.com. His site has a number of fantastic tools that will help you trim your monthly spending. I highly recommend you visit him, and while you are there, download this report: http://www.thesimpledollar.com/onepage/

SUMMARY

Chapter Seven: Get out of Debt

- Make a list of all of your debts.
- Determine which debt charges you the most interest.
- Consolidate your debt wisely to the lowest interest rate.
- Put all your effort into eliminating your highest-interest debt first, then tackle the rest.

Chapter Eight:
A Chat About Debt and Budgeting

I want to have a little heart-to-heart with you about budgeting. Get cozy. Light a candle. Put on some Sinatra.

You see, budgeting is the most important thing to do with respect to financial successes, but it's also the most difficult thing to do.

Why?

Because we want what we want when we want it.

We see that car, we want it. When you see that game on the schedule, you want to go. That concert? Great. The purse? Let's have it. But budgeting is grown-up behavior. It's saying, well, I want those things, but I'm not going to have them.

Some people use software to track spending. It's a very good way to look back and see where mistakes were made and what needs to be improved. Personally, I love the **Five Minutes a Month Method** -- much quicker and absolutely accurate. So if you're going to use software, it's no problem. Just make sure you also use the **Five Minutes a Month Method** to give you the overall picture.

Just a couple of tips on budget tools:

You can use anything. Mint, Quickbooks, BudgetPulse, YNAB.

If you're going to use software, make sure you use it religiously. But understand that software looks back. It simply tells you what happened (where you spent your money). If you want to have something that's going to help you going forward, to curb your spending, an envelope system might be really good.

What's the envelope system? That's just getting a few plain old envelopes and setting aside money in each for a specific category. You might have one envelope for entertainment, another for clothing and another for food. You put money in the envelopes at the beginning of the week or the beginning of the month, and then you take money out as needed. When the envelopes are empty, you don't buy anymore. You can't borrow from the next month.

The envelope system is excellent, and there are people at all stages of life and all economic levels who use envelopes to keep themselves under control.

Use the envelope system. And there's no shame in needing to use something like this.

You might think, "Oh, what am I, a child? I don't need to use this...."

But, it doesn't matter. If you need this kind of assistance, use it. For bigger items, you can set up electronic envelopes by putting money into different checking accounts or bank accounts. ING has special accounts that you can set up for different types of goals.

So software and envelopes are great. But the most important ingredient for financial success is to have a budgeting mentality.

I spoke about the problem of wanting what we want when we want it. This is the issue.

You can have all of the software and envelopes in the world. If you don't have the right budgeting mentality, it's not going to help you have financial success. It doesn't matter if you had bad role models or no role models while you were growing up.

It doesn't matter if you're in trouble or not right now. What happened in the past can't be undone. We have to move ahead. You do this by having an adult mentality.

What is the right mentality?

It's simply admitting that there will be times when a voice in your head will tell you to act like a child (with money) and you're not going to listen to that voice.

You're going to call your accountability partner instead and stay present. Your going to give that little voice a time-out and carry on. That's the right mentality and I know you can do it.

What Tools Will You Use to Help You Budget?

- Are you going to use envelopes?

- Is software going to be useful to you?

- Are you going to use the Five Minutes a Month Method?

- What is going to be the most powerful for you?

SUMMARY

Chapter Eight: A Chat About Debt and Budgeting

- Budgeting is the most important thing to do with respect to financial success, but also the most difficult.
- We prefer instant gratification to the discipline of budgeting our expenses. We want what we want when we want it.
- Budget tools like software or an envelopes system can help.

Chapter Nine:
Prioritize

Prioritization is often at the heart of our financial struggles. We ask ourselves and our partners, "How do we know which of our goals to go after and when?"

There's a great tool that can help you answer that question. It's called a decision matrix.

The decision matrix helps you answer that question, and I'm going to help you create your own matrix in this module.

This is a tool the Navy SEALS use.

Obviously the Navy SEALS need to be very focused on what they're doing. They need to keep their energy trained on their objectives rather than fighting about what their priorities are.

Think about a laser, which is very focused light, versus diffused light. A laser has lots of energy and is powerful. But a diffused light has little energy. It can't do anything.

I want you to focus all your energy on achieving your goals rather than fighting about them.

Here's how to do it.

Look at each of your goals and rank them according to six criteria.

The first criterion is how significant the goal is. How vital is it to you overall?

Second, how accessible is the goal? How easy will it be for you to get to it? Do you have the authority? If you make the effort, can you achieve your goal or do you depend on other people to get it done?

Next, how recognizable is it? Will you know what you need to do in order to get it done? Do you know what you need to do? Or is it all a mystery?

Fourth, is the target or the goal easy to achieve? Also, does your pursuit of the goal make your financial situation more vulnerable or stronger?

Fifth, how much will the achievement of this goal mean to you overall?

And finally, return on effort. Is it worth it?

What I'd like you to do now is create your matrix. It should look like this:

> Using one piece of paper, each person should write down their top three goals. We'll have one piece of paper with a total of six goals. (See the exercises for an example of the matrix you can use.)

Let's go through a few examples.

Here's the first goal. Steve wants to go to Chile this summer. Anna doesn't think that the trip to Chile is really vital to her. So she gives it a 3, but for Steve, it's really important, so he gives it a 5.

GOAL: Trip to Chile	Significant	Accessible	Recognizable	Vulnerable	Overall Impact	Return on Effort	Total
Anna	3	4	4	1	2	2	16
Steve	5	4	3	2	4	4	22

Next, is it accessible? How easy will it be to get it done? Steve and Anna provide their own answers.

Next, do they know what to do? Is it up to them or do they need permission from someone else?

They know what to do. They don't need anyone's permission in order to go to Chile. They just need to save money -- $250 each month. Steve and Anna rank how vulnerable the goal makes them next.

Does the pursuit of this goal make them stronger or weaker financially?

Well, to Anna, spending $3,000 on a trip to Chile makes them weaker. She feels this way because she has other goals which are much more important, and the trip to Chile would make it harder to achieve those goals. Steve recognizes that they have other financial issues as well. He realizes that spending $3,000 on Chile would make the couple more financially vulnerable. They each rank the vulnerability box with a low score.

Next is overall impact on happiness. It wouldn't be that important to Anna to go. But this is a lifelong dream for Steve.

Is it worth the effort? For Anna, it's not. She gives it a two but Steve gives it a four.

Having completed the exercise, the couple ads up the total score. Anna gives this goal a total of 16, while Steve gives it a 22. Together, the total is 38.

Keep in mind that your goals have to be measurable, both in amounts and in time. Break your financial goals down to dollar amounts needed per month. For example, let's say you have a retirement goal of saving $500,000 over the next 20 years. Break that down to an amount you need to save per month over 20 years in order to reach that goal. If, on the other hand, you just focus on saving $500,000 and ignore the time over which you're going to save that money, you'll put everything possible towards that goal. You'll do nothing else with your money. That's not a very balanced approach and it's certainly no fun.

Let's look at one more example so you see how Steve and Anna can use the matrix to prioritize.

The next goal is paying off the couple's credit card debt of $5,000 within 12 months.

For Anna, it's very significant. For Steve, it's also important.

Is it accessible? Their income is limited, so they rank it accordingly.

GOAL: Pay off credit card debt	Significant	Accessible	Recognizable	Vulnerable	Overall Impact	Return on Effort	Total
Anna	5	3	5	4	4	4	25
Steve	4	2	4	4	4	4	22

Recognizable: Do they know what they need to do? Yes. Anna gives it a 5 and Steve gives it a 4.

Vulnerable: They both recognized that by paying off that credit card debt, they will become financially stronger.

Overall Impact: Paying off the debt would make Anna very happy. It would make Steve happy too. First, he'd have peace of mind in knowing he was doing the right thing. Next, he'd know that his partner would be happier.

So the totals come to 25 for Anna and 22 for Steve. The grand total is 47. Let me remind you that the Chile trip totaled only 38. This means that the couple should put up to $450 towards their debts before saving money for the Chile trip.

See how easy that is?

Now it's your turn.

First, each of you should write down three goals on your matrix.

Next, each of you should rank the items.

Finally, calculate the totals and focus on the goal with the greatest score.

This is likely to be an eye opener for you.

The mistake that many of us make is to go after the easiest target first. We go for the low-hanging fruit. What this matrix will point out to you is that the easy targets may not be all that important to you.

You may learn that while certain goals may feel important, they may not be worth it, so they drop down on the priority scale.

This is a great way for you to communicate with your partner because you're going to see how each of you values joint goals. You'll learn why you value certain goals and not others.

Now, the reason this is so important is because people often spend lots of time on goals that aren't really that significant for them. My strong recommendation is that you look at the exercises you did earlier ("What's important about money to you?") to get ideas for your goals.

I also recommend discussing this with the entire family, and revisiting it every couple of months. Put it on your calendars now to come back and look at this to make sure you really stay focused on your goals. Are you working on those that are most important? Or have you slipped back to maybe things that aren't that important?

How To Prioritize

Directions: Complete this exercise together.

- Each person lists his/her three most important financial priorities

- How much money do you need to put aside each month in order to achieve that goal?

- Separately, fill out the enclosed "Priority Matrix"

- Combine your scores

- Order the priorities by highest to lowest

- Take action

Priority Matrix

GOAL	Significant	Accessible	Recognizable	Vulnerable	Overall Impact	Return on Effort	Total

SUMMARY

Chapter Nine: Prioritize

- Prioritization helps us know which goals to pursue first.
- A decision matrix can help with prioritization.
- Completing the matrix will help you and your partner communicate better and understand your values.

Chapter Ten:
Hiring a Financial Adviser

You or your spouse might consider hiring a financial adviser at some point. This is a critical decision. If you select the wrong advisor – or the right advisor, but have misguided expectations – it could lead to frustration, not to mention financial disaster.

Mistakes here could leave a mark.

So the questions are, do you need to hire adviser, and if so, who?

In order to answer these questions, you need some background information.

Understand the terrain.

Why?

Because the people who didn't bother to get this information before they made these decisions are the same ones who invested their life savings with Bernie Madoff – or a similar character. Unfortunately, many of those people lost everything they had.

I don't want that to happen to you, so please bear with me and really take note of what we're about to go through.

First, understand that there are two major oversight bodies when it comes to investments and investment advisors. The first is the SEC (Securities and Exchange Commission) and the other is the NASD (National Association of Securities

Dealers). The only thing that is important for you to understand is that the NASD isn't a government agency like the SEC. It's an industry watchdog created by financial industry fat cats. That might help you understand why some people feel they are more interested in protecting their own skins rather than your money.

Bottom line, it's up to you to protect your money, and by reading this section, I think you'll be much better able to do so.

In a few minutes, I'm going to explain how different financial advisers work, but for now, I want to give you and your partner some general guidelines. This is meant to keep you both on the same page – and safe.

1. **Don't let fancy credentials and high-flying reputations influence you.**

Do your own due diligence and investigation. It isn't that difficult, and it won't take you that long to do. I am going to spell out exactly what you can do to check out your adviser.

One of the reasons that Bernie Madoff got away with his crimes for so long was that people like you and me were convinced that Bernie was doing us a favor by taking our money.

We hire professionals largely based on referrals from friends … right?

Bernie took advantage of that.

He manufactured a wonderful reputation by providing influential people with very high returns. Of course, his clients didn't know what Madoff was up to. They just saw how much money they were making with Bernie. They spread the word, and before long, folks were clamoring to give Madoff their money to invest.

So before you hire an adviser, ask yourself why you are doing it. Do you trust this person? Why? Based on someone else's experience, or what you've found out about this person yourself? Is this adviser promising you returns that are significantly higher than what the market has returned? If so, beware.

This actually leads us to the next point.

2. Don't fool yourself.

Investing has risks. If someone shows you a track record that is so good it's hard to believe – don't believe it.

Of course, it's very possible that an adviser has a great year or a string of great years. But there are always trade-offs to investment approaches. If your prospective adviser did much better than the market in any one year, they probably did much worse than the market in another year. That's not a bad thing... it's just how investing works.

People who get taken by jerks like Madoff are those who want to have their cake and eat it too. They want to make lots of money on their investments and take no risk in doing so.

Of course, everyone wants this... but reasonable people understand that this is just not possible. You can invest in certain ways that will reduce your risk in bad years... but that's going to reduce your return in good years. There is no way around it. If you demand returns that are just not possible, you are setting yourself up to be taken advantage of by the first person who comes along and promises it to you.

3. Never give any financial adviser direct access to your money.

Ever wonder why the super-rich get super-soaked by financial advisers? It's because they violate this rule. Let me explain how this works and why you need to pay attention to this even if you aren't a movie star or world champion ice skater.

When you work with an honest financial adviser, they place your money with a third-party custodian (Schwab, Fidelity, TD Ameritrade are examples of custodians). If you have an adviser, they probably have a limited power of attorney on your accounts with the custodian. That limited power of attorney is something that you have to sign and it gives them the power to buy and sell securities on your behalf.

They can't withdraw money from your account. By law, the only person who can withdraw money from your account is you.

Usually, you can call your adviser and tell them to send you money from your account. In this case, the adviser usually has the right to call the custodian and tell them you need money and to issue you a check. But the check has to be made payable to you and has to be sent to your address of record. (This is one reason that you should never ever allow your broker to move in with you. Also, as a rule, they are terrible cooks and leave their socks on the floor.)

So while a limited power of attorney is OK, you should never give your broker or adviser a general power of attorney. If you do, they can sign your name and legally act as if they are you. A general power of attorney is basically a license to steal if placed in the wrong hands.

This is what trips up the rich people who get taken to the cleaners. They entrust their fortune to a business manager. That business manager has a general power of attorney. With that document, the business manager can clean out their clients' bank accounts and investments if they want to. Of course, most business managers are as honest as the day is long but you need to know the risks you take when you sign a general power of attorney.

Bottom line? Never give an adviser your money or access to your money. Any and all investments should be made by writing a check to a third-party custodian.

One other tip. When you deal with a broker or Registered Investment Adviser, they are usually precluded from asking you for a general power of attorney. It doesn't mean the rotten ones won't ask you for one, but at least there are added safeguards.

4. Get investment statements.

If you do nothing else, make sure you check (and understand) your investment statements every month. This is the simplest and most effective thing you can do to make sure you don't get taken advantage of.

Again, your statements should come from a third-party custodian. Your adviser can send you statements every month, quarter or year. No problem.

But you must also insist on getting monthly statements directly from the custodian, no matter what. If you don't get monthly statements from the custodian, you have no way of knowing what's going on with your account – or even if it still exists.

What's to keep a super-slimy adviser from printing up his own statements?

Nothing.

It's been done before. That's why you should take the extra precaution of calling your custodian every few months and confirming your balances directly with them.

By the way, if you do this, and I hope you will, make sure to look up the phone number independently. If your adviser is printing up his own statements, chances are high that he'll fabricate a phone number, too. Make sure you take this all-important step.

Having said that, there are a few types of investments that don't allow you to take these precautions. If you invest in real estate partnerships and/or hedge funds, there is no third-party custodian involved (in most cases). The only statements you will get from these types of investments will be from your adviser. This is why much of the fraud that takes place usually involves limited partnerships and hedge funds.

For this reason alone, I shy away from investing in these alternatives. Of course, this is not to say that every limited partnership and hedge fund is a snake pit. I'm just saying that you have much less security and oversight when you invest in either one.

To summarize what we've learned so far, there are a number of very simple steps you can take that will safeguard you and your money.

Simple steps to safeguard you and your money.

1. Don't invest with someone based on reputation alone.
2. Don't fool yourself. Understand how investments work.
3. Never give your adviser direct access to your money.
4. Get third-party investment statements.

With these guidelines in mind, let's learn about how different advisers work:

There is one cardinal rule that you both must really "get" before you hire an adviser:

> The type of license an advisor has determines what kind of financial advice he/she can give you.

That means when your advisor gives you a solution, it could simply be the only product that particular advisor is able to sell.

Let's start out by discussing the CFP® (Certified Financial Planner) designation.

The CFP® designation is not a license. It has no impact whatsoever on which investment products the CFP can or cannot suggest to you the client.

The CFP® designation is highly regarded within the professional community. In order to qualify for the designation, there are education, experience, ethics and examination requirements.

I'm not going to go through all the requirements, but they are relatively vigorous -- at least that was my experience when I became a certified financial planner 15 years ago. I had to study pretty hard for two years to pass exams in six subjects (I believe it has been reduced to five subjects now). After I passed the six exams, I had to sit for a two-day comprehensive exam.

I didn't find the course of study all that educational, but given the choice of hiring an adviser who is a CFP and another who is not, I'd suggest you go with the CFP. It's the most comprehensive designation out there that I am aware of. It demonstrates commitment.

Also, the designation creates fiduciary responsibility to clients.

In other words, your CFP must put your financial interests first. If a CFP knowingly acts in any other way, he/she breaks that fiduciary responsibility and can lose the designation. This doesn't guarantee that every CFP you meet is going to be Mother Teresa with an adding machine, but it does set a higher standard.

Bottom line – the CFP is a great designation. It demonstrates commitment, the need for comprehensive planning and the supreme importance of putting clients' needs first.

Does it mean your CFP knows how to manage money? No.

Does it mean your CFP knows how to put a financial plan together? Not really. It's just a good starting place.

Let's move on to talk about people who make a living telling you what to do with your money.

Let's see if we can learn more about how advisers are licensed, trained and compensated to find someone you can trust.

Consider fee-based planners.

Enter, if you will, the world of the Registered Investment Adviser (RIA).

If someone charges a fee to provide financial advice, they must become a Registered Investment Adviser.

Registered Investment Advisers don't work on commissions. They work for fees. Either they charge you an hourly fee, a fee for a project (like creating your financial plan) or a fee for assets they manage for you.

Registered Investment Advisers are either registered with the SEC (if they manage over $25 million) or with the state they operate in (if they manage under $25 million).

The difference between RIA's, insurance agents and stockbrokers is that RIA's don't charge commissions for their work. They can't.

What's the difference between a fee and a commission -- it still costs money, right?

True. But when I pay someone a commission to sell me a widget, I don't know if he sold me that widget because he makes the most commission on it or because he really, really cares about me like he seems to.

If I pay someone a fee to represent me, he theoretically has no interest other than making sure I get the best widget there is. Of course it doesn't always work out this way, but you have better odds of working with someone who is partial to you if you work with a fee-based planner.

How does one become a Registered Investment Adviser?

You take a few tests and fill out some paperwork. Not a huge deal. In my opinion, this process does nothing to guarantee qualifications. It doesn't speak to expertise or trustworthiness.

A Registered Investment Adviser often works in a small office with maybe two or three associates. However, some large firms do exist. The reason this is important to you as a client is that you want to make sure you get unbiased advice. If you work with an adviser from a large firm, you're more likely to get advice that has been filtered through the top people at the firm. Typically, the smaller the firm, the more independent your adviser will be. This of course can work for or against you, but it's just nice to know who is really calling the shots.

(Disclaimer: I am a Registered Investment Adviser and I work in a small office. I work this way because it suits me and my clients, but I clearly have a bias. I have tried to take my bias out of this while being honest about my experience at the same time, but take it in with a grain of salt.)

For my money, you want to be sitting across the table with the person who is making the recommendations. I don't want an order clerk masquerading as a financial adviser and neither do you.

So the benefits of using a Registered Investment Adviser is that she is not beholden to a large management infrastructure (if she works for a small firm). But while this can be a benefit, it also reduces the scrutiny the adviser is subject to.

Who oversees RIA's?

Once in awhile, the SEC or Department of Corporations will come in and audit the RIA firm but this is by no means any guarantee that the firm you are working with is above board.

I already mentioned one example of when the SEC missed a small problem: Bernie Madoff.

Bernie was a Registered Investment Adviser, and the SEC was supposed to be auditing him. Oops.

Bernie got away with being the biggest shyster of all time – at least so far. To be fair, being a Registered Investment Adviser helped him get away with theft for a long time, but it really wasn't the main reason he was able to perpetrate his evil fraud.

How did Bernie do it?

RIA's usually manage money for people at a large custodian like TD Ameritrade, Fidelity or Schwab. This is important because it creates a "firewall" between the adviser and your money. If an adviser tries to steal money from an account at Fidelity, for example, you'll see it because Fidelity sends you statements. The use of a custodian is an important safeguard for you.

But Bernie didn't do that. He formed limited partnerships and hedge funds. These entities have almost no scrutiny by outside authorities – and they don't send you third-party statements. It's a black box – and it can be sort of like that old roach killer commercial.

Your money checks in…but never checks out. Yikes!

Sometimes, other professionals use these same set-ups to rip off their clients. CPA's, business managers and lawyers also get caught with their hands in the cookie jar. So, it's not so much that RIA's are the risk -- it's these types of investments that can be treacherous.

Let's move on to insurance agents and stockbrokers.

If you've never seen the movie "Groundhog Day" with Bill Murray, you should rent it.

There is a scene where Murray's character confronts an old acquaintance who is now an insurance agent. This shyster tries every trick in the book to get Murray to buy life insurance. I won't tell you how he turns the tables on the salesman but that scene alone is worth the rental price.

Insurance agents have a bum rap, and I hate to say it, but much of it is for a good reason in my opinion.

The State issues licenses to sell insurance. If someone only has an insurance license, they can only sell -- you guessed it -- insurance.

Such a person is likely to see life insurance as the solution to whatever your financial problems are.

Life insurance agents are either captive or independent. A captive life insurance agent is only allowed to sell the insurance products that her insurance company sells. That means if you are talking to a captive Met Life agent, he can only sell those products that Met Life approves of.

By the way, they don't call them agents for nothing. These people are agents for the companies they work for – they are not your agents.

If you are dealing with an independent agent, she can sell insurance products from a variety of insurance companies.

But the main point is that if your financial adviser only has an insurance license, he can only and will only sell you insurance products.

Am I saying that life insurance is bad? Am I saying that nobody needs life insurance? No I am not.

What I am saying however is that life insurance is one piece of the puzzle that you may or may not need. I am also saying that most people I know have financial needs that life insurance can't meet. So yes, you might need some life insurance, and no, life insurance can't solve all your financial problems.

Life insurance agents sometimes tell you that whole or universal life is a tool that will help you save for retirement. Don't fall for it. The only people I've ever seen benefit from the sale of these products are the people who sell them.

If your financial adviser is only licensed as a life insurance agent, you should find a new adviser – even if your current adviser is your brother.

What about stockbrokers?

Like insurance agents, stockbrokers work for their employer – not you. Their first responsibility is to the brokerage firm.

Does this mean that every stockbroker is a dirty rotten scoundrel? Nope. You've got to compare brokers. Some of my closest friends are stockbrokers. Most of the stockbrokers I've met really want to do the best they can for their clients. The only problem I have with these folks is that they are held accountable first and foremost to their firms and not to their clients.

Their firm decides what they can and can't sell. Their firms decides how much commission the broker will get if that broker sells product A as opposed to product B. This is a huge conflict of interest, and it's the reason I left the brokerage business many years ago.

I was a stockbroker for a very large bank in California. My manager wanted me to sell more annuities (a life insurance product) to clients because the commissions were higher. I didn't want to do it because I thought they were a bad deal for my clients, and this led to a problem.

My manager's constituents were his bosses, and he wanted to make them happy. My constituents were my clients. If I didn't make them happy, I would be out of business. I could not maximize my clients' interests without jeopardizing the interests of my manager, so I split.

And lots of brokers are leaving the brokerage world for that exact reason. My point is that if you are still working with a broker, you are at a disadvantage. Your broker makes recommendations to you only after his employer has given the green light. That's like a doctor having to get permission from the pharmaceutical companies before he can subscribe any medication. That just plain stinks.

Pulling it all together.

Everything you now know about financial advisers is worth less than gum on the bottom of your shoe unless you understand this one simple fact:

Many (if not most) advisers have multiple licenses and designations. This complicates what you can expect from your adviser, and it makes lots of room for unintentional misunderstanding.

Let's use a few examples to illustrate how important this is.

Assume you are talking with a (captive or otherwise) insurance agent who is also a CFP® but has no other licenses or registrations.

You might expect him to live up the CFP's fiduciary responsibility requirement. You'd expect him to put your interests above his own or his firm's interests. That would be reasonable...

Except it can't happen.

Remember? If this person only has an insurance license, they can only sell insurance products. Can anyone possibly think that life insurance is the answer to all your financial needs? It ain't.

To make matters worse, a captive insurance agent works for the insurance company. We've gone over that already. He'll sell what the insurance company tells him to sell – regardless of being a CFP®.

How does that square with the responsibilities of being a CFP®?

In my opinion, it doesn't. I can't understand how an insurance agent is allowed to be a CFP® but much to my surprise the CFP board hasn't asked for my opinion on the matter, so we'll just move on.

Why is this important to you?

Because when this insurance agent holds himself out to you as being a CFP®, you have a reasonable expectation of dealing with someone who will be a champion for your interests. That's what being a CFP® is supposed to mean in my opinion.

There is an inherent conflict between being an agent for an employer (insurance agent or brokerage firm) and holding yourself out to the public as being a fiduciary. It doesn't work, and it's dangerous for you as an investor to think someone is a fiduciary when in fact they are not.

Some stockbrokers can also have an insurance license. They can sell you investments and insurance. This is very common and doesn't present any inherent conflict.

But it gets complicated when an insurance agent and/or stockbroker is a Registered Investment Adviser or associated with an RIA firm. They do this in order to charge consulting fees and/or manage money for you.

This can bring up conflicts of interest similar to those mentioned above when the broker also has a CFP® designation.

A Registered Investment Adviser also has a fiduciary responsibility to the client but how can she deliver on that if she is primarily beholden to her brokerage or insurance company? I just don't see how she can do it.

The bottom line is that many advisers wear many hats. You just have to be sure of which hat they are wearing when you talk to them.

Do I think that advisers intentionally become a CFP® in order to lull you into a false sense of security before they rip you off? I do not.

I think most pursue this designation with honorable intentions. It's just that once they do have the designations, certain advisers just can't adhere to the duties associated with the designation because of whom they work for. That's the dangerous part for you.

There is one simple way to make sure these complications won't hurt you.

Ask your adviser the following question:

"How does being a CFP or Registered Investment Adviser influence the advice you've just given me?"

No matter whom you are dealing with, or what licenses or designations they hold, this is the best question you can ask to get clarity on whom you are really dealing with.

The answer should include some mention of impartiality...

Pay attention to your gut. If the answer sounds like a bunch of hogwash, move on.

Now that we've gone over how financial advisers work, the question becomes: Do you need one?

I don't think that everyone needs a financial adviser. I really don't.

Deciding whether or not you need an adviser is fairly simple.

The question is: What do you want to achieve?

Do you need life insurance? The Internet will give you the most competitive quotes.

If your problem is spending and debt, you shouldn't need an adviser to help you with that after going through the material presented in Money Academy.

If you still want to talk to someone, by all means go ahead. Just be very clear about what you want, and look for someone you can pay on an hourly basis. If you go to an insurance agent to talk about your budget challenges, you're going to leave with an insurance policy – whether you need one or not.

For needs like these, I would recommend an RIA who is also a CFP.

Do you feel directionless? Get yourself a good financial plan. This should cost no more than $500 to $850. Again, the CFP who is also an RIA would be a good bet.

Are you looking for investment ideas? You might be able to manage your money by yourself. There are a number of great books on this subject.

If you do want to hire a money manager, a stockbroker or RIA might work for you.

Just make sure that you understand where they are coming from before turning over your hard earned money.

I've spent a great deal of time on this subject for two very simple reasons:

1. The type of advisor you hire will significantly impact your overall financial situation.

2. If you understand how advisers work, you'll have fewer arguments about how to select the right one (if you need one).

SUMMARY

Chapter Ten: Hiring a Financial Adviser

- Selecting the wrong financial advisor can lead to frustration and financial mishap.
- Don't be fooled by an advisor's high-flying reputation.
- Never give an advisor direct access to your money.
- The type of license an advisor has determines what kind of financial advice he/she can give you.

Bonus Chapter:
Fire Yourself

You've learned a lot together so far, and I'm about to give you a bonus module that's going to make the program much more powerful than it otherwise would be. You've earned it.

But let's see what we've learned so far.

First, you're in this together. You and your partner both want to have a happier relationship and a better financial situation. You're both on the same page, and you're willing to have open, honest discussions about how to improve your situation.

Second, you learned how to track your spending in five minutes a month. This is the single most important thing you can do. It's easy and fun.

Third, "dollarize" your behavior. See what your pastimes and hobbies really cost you in terms of time and money.

Fourth, we talked about how to find common ground. Understand what it is that's financially important to your partner and also what might be bugging them about your financial behavior. This will help you understand your partner better. It will also help you avoid reacting negatively and taking things personally.

Fifth, stop digging into debt, right?

Sixth, we talked about how to get out of debt.

Lastly, we talked about budgeting, prioritization, and hiring a financial advisor.

Now, let's look at the one obstacle still remaining.

All you have to do is look in the mirror. Yes…that's right. The remaining obstacle is you.

You may have heard some of what we've discussed in this book before. You may have made past promises to yourself or others that you'd do something.

You may already know what to do….so I have one question.

Why is it that you haven't taken action?

The reason is because we get in our own way. Even though we know we need to do things differently, a voice in our head tells us to give it another try.

So what is the solution?

Honesty.

The solution is honesty.

We have character flaws.

On one hand, we tell ourselves that we really need to do something. Another part of us tells us we want what we want when we want it. Or that we're right and everyone else is wrong.

We all have these little insidious voices inside that give us very bad advice. We listen to those voices, and they get us into trouble.

For example: I know I shouldn't be eating chocolate, but on a Friday night, when there's a really nice dessert, that little voice in my head says, "Maybe you could have some."

Mistake!

When you're walking by the store and you see that pair of shoes or outfit or concert tickets, you get tempted.

You know that you're in debt and you can't afford it. But that little voice inside you says, "Go ahead and do it."

And that's what we have to defeat. We have to defeat that little voice.

Let me tell you something - when you do defeat that little voice, you'll have 95% of your financial difficulties licked.

How do you do that?

Well, basically, you have to fire yourself.

Think about it.

What would you do with an employee who continually blew it? Wouldn't you fire him? Of course you would.

Assume they were in charge of budgeting and they continued to go over their budget. Or they were in charge of getting supplies together and they never did it. Whenever you came into the supply room, it was empty. What would you do with that person? You would fire them.

Well, I want you to fire yourself for the same reasons. You're not a loser, but your best thinking has gotten you where you are now. And if you were satisfied with your current situation, you wouldn't have gone through this course.

Keep in mind that I'm not talking about firing your spouse. I'm talking about you.

You've got to fire yourself from some sphere of responsibility and hire someone else.

Now, what do I mean by that?

Basically, you're going to put someone else in charge. (Don't worry, I'm not telling you to hire a financial adviser necessarily).

How?

In order to fire yourself, you have to ask yourself a few questions:

1. What part of your financial behavior do you most want to change?
2. Is there something that you've tried to change in the past, but weren't able to?
3. Why do you want to change it?
4. How does that financial behavior impact your financial life and your relationship with your partner?

This is part of your homework. You need to go through this exercise. It's painful and you may not want to do this work. But let's review why you are doing this.

You are "firing yourself" because you have demonstrated a complete lack of ability to control some aspect of your financial life. You've promised yourself that you would stop some behavior. You've tried to stop, but you can't.

So who is going to take over?

That's easy – and very inexpensive. You are either going to cede control of this one aspect of your life to your spouse or an accountability partner.

I spoke about accountability partners before.

An accountability partner is someone who has what you want to have in terms of control over finances. Your accountability partner doesn't have to be the wealthiest person in the world, but he or she has to be someone who is financially balanced, financially joyful and at peace. That's who you're looking for and who you want as an accountability partner. It might be your spouse or partner, but it might not be. It's someone you trust.

For example, if you decide that you're going to fire yourself from buying baseball game tickets, I suggest that you report in to your accountability partner every week. It might sound juvenile at first. But ultimately, it's going to help you grow up financially. Why?

Because when we act like children when it comes to money, it's about not wanting to grow up. Having an accountability partner basically solves that problem. Sometimes, the accountability partner acts like the adult you are unwilling to be for yourself. Other times, you act like an adult simply because you don't want to have to tell your accountability partner about all the bone-heads things you've done.

What I'd like you to do now is go through the exercise.

Identify those things that you need to fire yourself over in your financial life. Find an accountability partner. Talk to them. Put them in charge. Do the homework. And please, most importantly, communicate with your partner.

Fire Yourself

Directions: Complete this exercise individually and discuss.

1. What part of your financial behavior do you most want to change?

2. Why?

3. How does that behavior impact your financial life and relationships?

4. What have you done in the past to try to control it?

5. What has been the result?

6. Who are you going to "hire"?

7. How will you remember?

8. Are you going to write up a "contract" between you and your accountability partner? What will it spell out? When are you going to do this?

SUMMARY

Bonus Chapter: Fire Yourself

- When we know that we need extra help to make sure we're staying within our boundaries, it can help to have an accountability partner.
- An accountability partner is someone you trust (it can be your spouse or someone else) who will keep you honest about your financial behavior.
- Work with your partner to:
  - ▷ Set ground rules;
  - ▷ Do weekly updates;
  - ▷ Update monthly spreadsheets;
  - ▷ And establish savings or other goals.

Conclusion

In conclusion, you should feel great about what you've done so far. You have gone through the modules and done the exercises. You've discussed the results, and hopefully, you've seen the results of some of the changes you've implemented.

I strongly encourage you to come back to these modules every six months. It won't take you that long and it's a great way for you to make sure you're still on track.

I would absolutely love to hear about your successes. Please send me an email at **nfrankle@pacbell.net**. Let me know how you've done, what you're still struggling with and how I can improve this course.

I strongly encourage you to get free updates from my blog. You can visit me there at www.wealthpilgrim.com. I write about these and other topics extensively and I hope you join the community –it's free.

In the meantime, I wish you success and congratulate you again for all the progress you've made so far.

Neal

Breinigsville, PA USA
02 April 2010
235407BV00005B/28/P